YOUR BACKPACK EXPLORER STICKER

Nature is ALL AROUND YOU!

With this sticker book, you can learn the names of more than 100 **BUGS, TREES, FLOWERS, REPTILES, AMPHIBIANS, BIRDS,** and **MAMMALS.**

Look at the **ACTIVITY PAGES,** then find the **STICKERS** in the back of the book.

MATCH THE STICKERS to the pictures . . .

and **MAKE YOUR OWN FIELD GUIDE** to bring outside!

I SEE BUGS!

The world is full of all kinds of amazing bugs and other creepy crawlers. You can find them buzzing, flying, climbing, and crawling nearly anywhere! Match up the stickers from the back of the book to the pictures below.

Honeybee

Grasshopper

Dragonfly

House cricket

Notice the shape, size, and color of a bug to help you identify it.

Pill bug

Monarch butterfly

Yellow garden spider

Potato beetle

Ants

Millipede

Water bugs

Housefly

Bumblebee

Stinkbug

Wolf spider

Moth

Daddy longlegs

Damselfly

Ladybug

Paper wasp

Go outside and peek in flowers, check under logs, and look in shallow water to find bugs!

Praying mantis

Centipede

I SEE TREES!

Look at all the trees around you. Notice the differences in their shapes and in their leaves and needles. Now match the stickers to the pictures of trees below.

There are two kinds of trees: deciduous and coniferous.

Sycamore

Crab apple

Douglas fir

Coast redwood

Oaks, maples, and other deciduous trees lose their leaves in the autumn.

Oak

White birch

Horse chestnut

Conifers have needles and cones.

Blue spruce

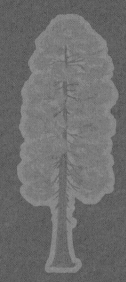
Incense cedar

Pine

Larch

Ginkgo

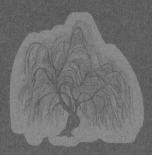
Weeping wlllow

Apple

Quaking aspen

Southern magnolia

Giant sequoia

I SEE FLOWERS!

Flowers grow in so many different colors, shapes, and sizes. Some flowering plants grow many blossoms on each stem. Others have just one head per stem. Match the stickers to the pictures below.

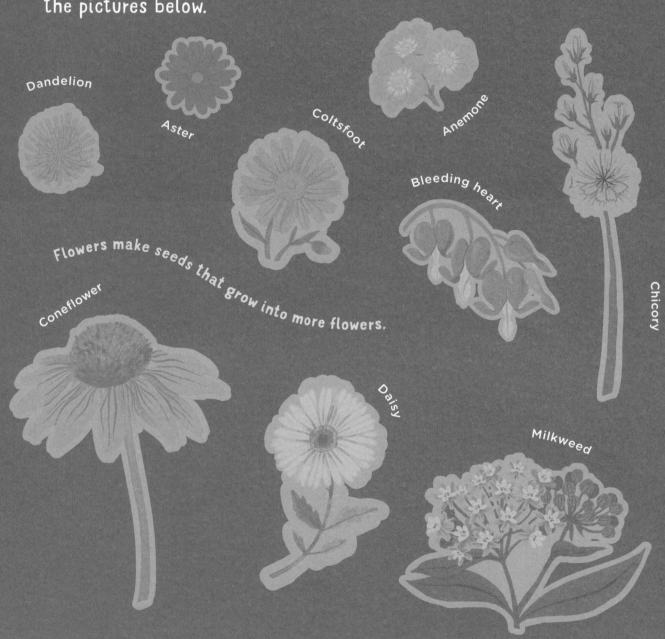

Dandelion

Aster

Coltsfoot

Anemone

Bleeding heart

Chicory

Flowers make seeds that grow into more flowers.

Coneflower

Daisy

Milkweed

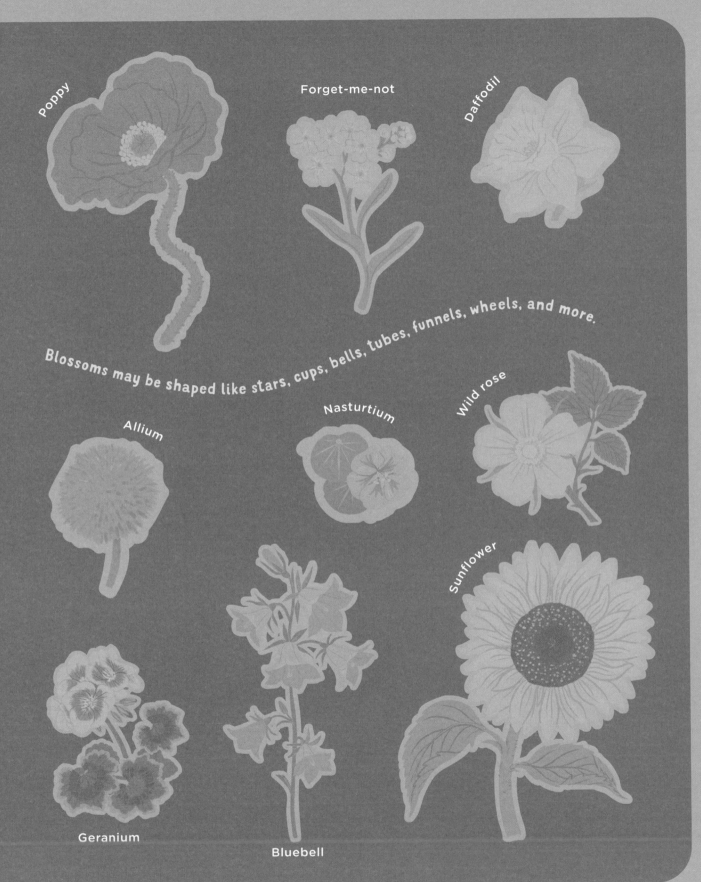

Poppy

Forget-me-not

Daffodil

Blossoms may be shaped like stars, cups, bells, tubes, funnels, wheels, and more.

Allium

Nasturtium

Wild rose

Sunflower

Geranium

Bluebell

I SEE MAMMALS!

Keep your eye out for furry animals big and small. Match the stickers to the pictures below.

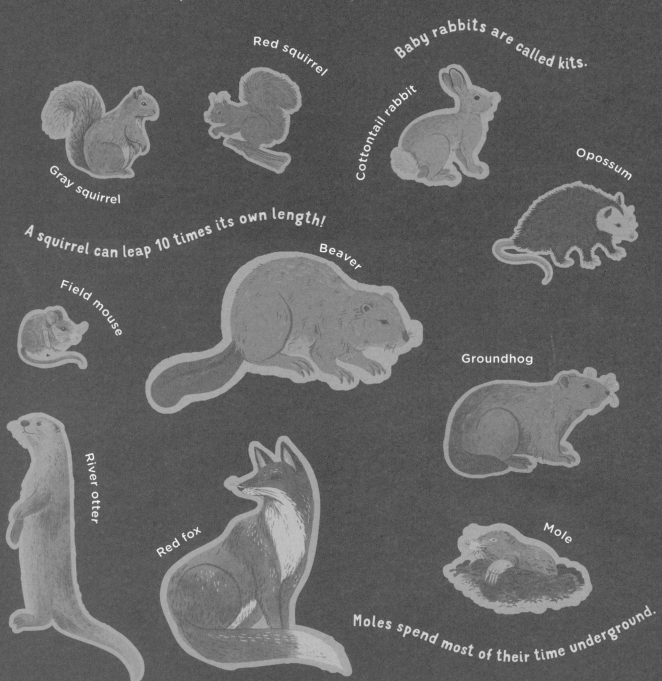

Red squirrel

Baby rabbits are called kits.

Cottontail rabbit

Opossum

Gray squirrel

A squirrel can leap 10 times its own length!

Field mouse

Beaver

Groundhog

River otter

Red fox

Mole

Moles spend most of their time underground.

Coyote

Carnivores, such as wolves, mostly eat meat.
(Most carnivores eat plants, too.)

Gray wolf

Herbivores, such as deer, eat only plants.

White-tailed deer

Chipmunk

Porcupine

Raccoon

Black bear

Skunk

Some animals, like bears, are omnivores—they eat both plants and meat.

I SEE BIRDS!

Although they come in many colors and shapes, all birds have feathers and lay eggs. Learn the names of some birds below, then find the stickers that match.

Red-headed woodpecker

Can you spot a nest among the tree branches nearby?

Common yellowthroat

Blue jay

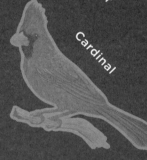

Cardinal

Most birds have hollow bones that make their bodies light enough to fly.

Mourning dove

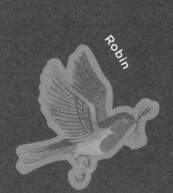

Robin

Raven

Barn
swallow

Goldfinch

Great horned owl

Can you find a bird soaring in the sky?

Red-tailed hawk

Chickadee

Peregrine falcon

Rufous
hummingbird

Whistling
ducks

Canada goose

Do you see any birds foraging for seeds, insects, or nectar?

Eurasian tree sparrow

I SEE AMPHIBIANS & REPTILES!

Frogs, toads, and salamanders are amphibians. Snakes, turtles, and lizards are reptiles. Match the stickers to the creatures below.

Eastern newt

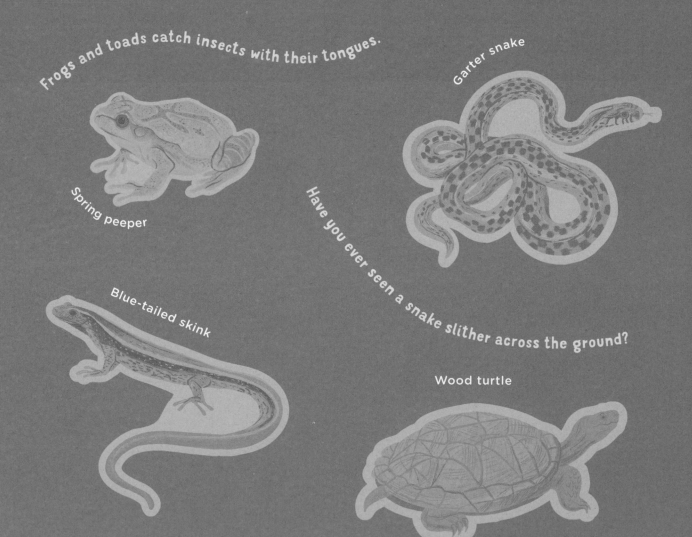

Frogs and toads catch insects with their tongues.

Garter snake

Spring peeper

Have you ever seen a snake slither across the ground?

Blue-tailed skink

Wood turtle

Look for amphibian eggs and tadpoles in a pond in the spring.

Box turtle

Tadpoles

Green frog

Listen for frog and toad calls.

Corn snake
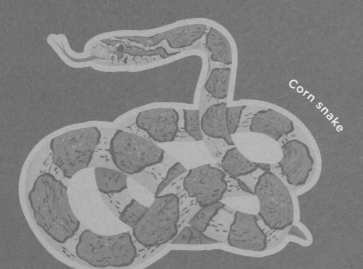

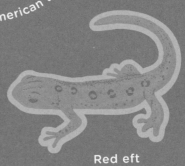
American toad

Red eft

Reptiles and amphibians are cold-blooded and depend on the sun to keep warm!

Horned lizard

Tiger
salamander

A Day at the Pond

Wetlands, like swamps and marshes, are habitats where much of the ground is wet or covered in water.

Sticker this scene with animals and birds who live in a wetland habitat.

WHAT IS A HABITAT?

A **habitat** is a place where plants and animals live. A good habitat provides food, water, and shelter.

Deep in the Forest

A forest, or woodland, is an area of land that is mostly made up of trees.

Sticker this scene with animals who live in a forest habitat.

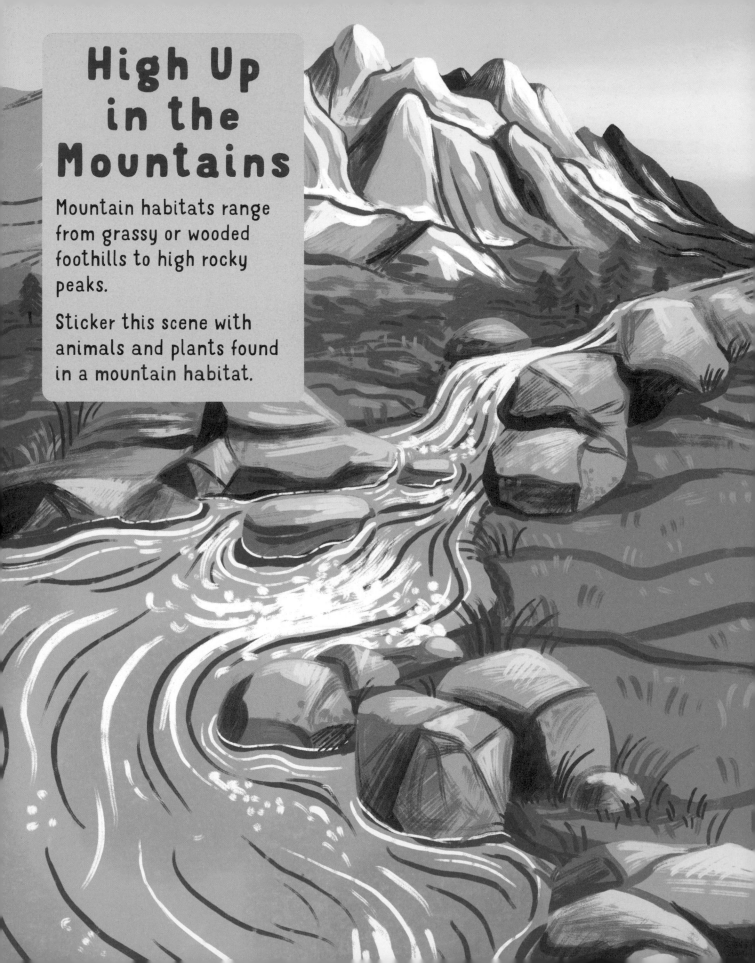

High Up in the Mountains

Mountain habitats range from grassy or wooded foothills to high rocky peaks.

Sticker this scene with animals and plants found in a mountain habitat.

Out in the Meadow

A meadow is an open, flat area covered in tall grass and wildflowers.

Sticker this scene with animals and plants that live in a meadow habitat.

Create Your Own Trail Map

Design a map of a nature adventure!

Use stickers to add plants and wildlife along the trail.

Use **arrows** to show the trail direction.

Along the way, add stickers of landmarks, such as a **fallen log** or a **big boulder**.

Add a **picnic table** or a **campfire ring**.

Add **wildlife** and a **mountain peak**.

Add a **bridge** to cross a stream.

START YOUR
TRAIL HERE

START

THE WEATHER
TODAY IS . . .

MARK THE END
OF YOUR TRAIL

END

Backpack Explorer

Grab your backpack and look for nature finds outside.
When you spot a flower, tree, bird, mammal, bug, amphibian, or
reptile, place a nature patch sticker on this backpack!

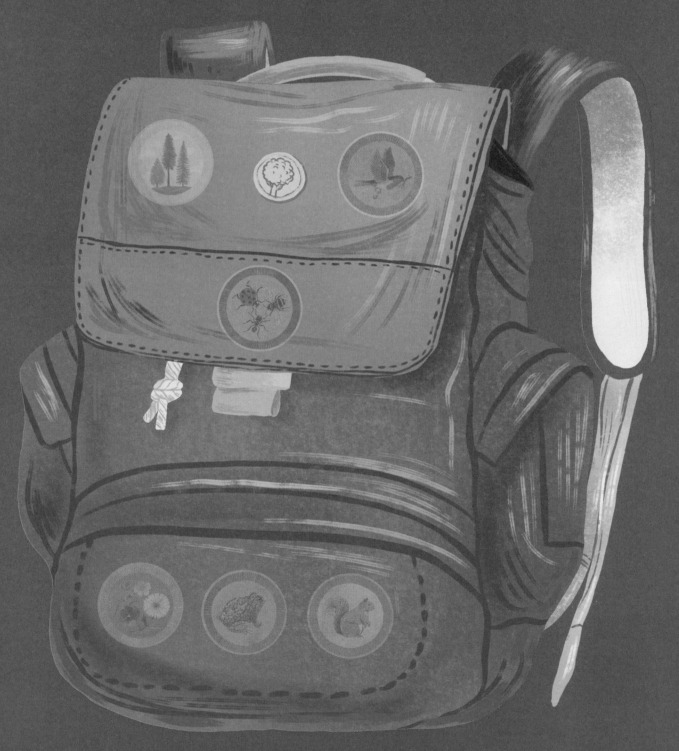